Icarus

Favourite Love Poems
By Wayne Visser

Second Edition

Second paperback edition published in 2016 by Kaleidoscope Futures, London, UK.

First paperback edition published in 2013 by Wayne Visser. First and second electronic edition published in 2013 by Wayne Visser and in 2016 by Kaleidoscope Futures.

Copyright © 2016 Wayne Visser.

All rights reserved. No part of this publication may be reproduced, stored in a retrieval system, or transmitted, in any form or by any means, electronic, mechanical, photocopying, recording or otherwise, except as permitted by the UK Copyright, Designs and Patents Act 1988, without the prior permission of the publisher.

Cover photography and design by Wayne Visser. Cover photograph of the author by Indira Kartallozi.

Printing and distribution by Lulu.com.

ISBN 978-1-908875-29-7

Dedication

To Indira, the love of my life. We may have ventured too close to the sun a few times, but we are still flying high.

Fiction Books by Wayne Visser

I Am An African: Favourite Africa Poems

Wishing Leaves: Favourite Nature Poems

Seize the Day: Favourite Inspirational Poems

String, Donuts, Bubbles and Me: Favourite Philosophical Poems

African Dream: Inspiring Words & Images from the Luminous Continent

Icarus: Favourite Love Poems

Life in Transit: Favourite Travel & Tribute Poems

Non-fiction Books by Wayne Visser

Beyond Reasonable Greed

South Africa: Reasons to Believe

Corporate Citizenship in Africa

Business Frontiers

The A to Z of Corporate Social Responsibility

Making A Difference

Landmarks for Sustainability

The Top 50 Sustainability Books

The World Guide to CSR

The Age of Responsibility

The Quest for Sustainable Business

Corporate Sustainability & Responsibility

CSR 2.0

Disrupting the Future

This is Tomorrow

Sustainable Frontiers

The CSR International Research Compendium

The World Guide to Sustainable Enterprise

About the Author

Wayne Visser was born in Zimbabwe and has lived most of his life in South Africa and the UK. He is a writer, academic, social entrepreneur, professional speaker and amateur artist.

Wayne is no stranger to the agonies and ecstasies of love – from careful planting to painful pruning; from first blush to full bloom. His views on love are best summed up in his own words:

Only love -

> *It's all that matters, all that binds*
> *All that fulfils, all that finds*
> *It's all that holds, all that contains*
> *All that is, all that remains*
>   *- Only love*

Website: www.waynevisser.com
Email: wayne@waynevisser.com

Contents

Icarus	1
Sky Dream	3
Enchanted	4
Fly to Love	5
Almost Strangers	6
Valentine	7
Perfume	8
The Web	10
Florentine Nights	11
Autumn Kisses	12
Love Floats	13
Ivy Love	14
The Dream of You	15
Perfect Day	16
Chocolate Seduction	17
A Love That Could Last	19
Galaxies Cart-Wheeling	21
I Hear You	22
Turkish Coffee Kisses	24
Flibbawookie	25
Broken Dreams	26
Love-Shapes	28

Just Imagine	29
Island Dreams	31
Listen As She Hums	33
The End (This Time)	34
Caterpillar Kisses	35
My Secret	36
Happy to See You	37
Scattered Leaves	38
Rainbow Mists	40
Talk to Me!	41
The Web of Love	42
Gifts	44
Dance Me	49
Gentle On My Mind	51
Dressing Gown	54
Desert Love	55
Subway Angel	57
Unspoken Words	58
Wild Love	60
Kismet	63
I Lie Awake	65
The Joining of Hands	66
Moment of Truth	68
Resonance	72
Ambivalence	73

Villanelle for Justice	74
Hard to Say	76
Through It All	78
Shooting Star	82
Step Into My Parlour	83
Footprints	84
Dove on the Wind	85
Reach Out and Touch	86
Only Love	87
Mystery	88
I Love You Mom	89
Dad, We Love You	90
Kindred Spirits	92
Hunny-Bear	93
Christmas Wish	94
Jealousy	95
Cradled by Love	97
Facets	98
Wild, Beautiful and Free	100
Truth or Dare	102
Genie Out the Bottle	104
Restless Nights	108
Letting Go	109
Princess	111
She'll Never Know	113

All I Ever Wanted	116
Here	118
If You Love Her	120
Battle Days	122
Finally Over	123
Two Weeks	125
Sad and Blue	127
Hope	130
Comet Sonnet	131
Adultery	132
Love Letter	134
Don't Tell Me That You Love Me	137
Lingerie Lament	139
Afterglow	140
Je T'Adore	142
Say "I Do!"	144
Love Is …	146
With This Ring	148
My Letters	149

Icarus

You've given me the gift of golden wings
The endless sphere of blue imaginings
The chance to rise above the silver clouds
The will to cast off untold ghostly shrouds

Don't fly too high
Don't rise too fast
Don't tease the sky
Don't taunt the past

You've given me the hope of warmer days
The blessed kiss of the sun's fiery rays
The breeze to fan passion's spark to a fire
The slow burning coals of glowing desire

Don't get too near
Don't burn too hot
Don't play with fear
Don't tempt your lot

You've given me the seed of unborn dreams
The fairy tale of "once upon a time"
The wish to ride bare back on white moon beams
The spell to enchant beauty's hidden rhyme

Sky Dream

A moon beam to brush your cheek
A star burst to lift your eyes
A sun ray to touch your lips
A bird song to greet your rise

A wind gust to clear your head
A cloud wisp to thread your sighs
A rain drop to quench your heart
A snow flake to soothe your cries

A rose bud to kiss your nose
A tree top to bless your highs
A duck pond to cast your wish
A sky dream to loose your ties

Enchanted

By the dream, I'm enchanted
By the fantasy, enticed
Who needs feet firmly planted
When the sky's laced with spice?

And yet what if we wake up
And find our passion tree bare
With just words left to rake up
Of what was budding and rare?

And yet we must take this chance
And walk the bridge of meeting
For only then can we dance
And feel each other breathing

Fly to Love

To fly
you must be free
To be free
you must let go
To let go
you must find trust
To find trust
you must have faith
To have faith
you must keep hope
To keep hope
you must see beauty
To see beauty
you must know love
To know love
you must learn to fly

The lesson is this:
If you love to fly
you must fly to love

Almost Strangers

The first time that we met
We were almost strangers – yet
When we smiled and parted
We went our separate ways

In between fate intervened
So that our paths could cross once more

The next time that we met
We were almost good friends – yet
When we kissed and parted
We held each other's gaze

All the while life's hidden smile
Knew that we'd reach this distant shore

When we next meet I'll bet
We'll be almost lovers – yet
We'll know that we've just started
The story of our days

Valentine

Don't give me hearts or scarlet blooms
No Hallmark cards or lovers' tunes
But kiss my cheek and hold my hand
Or trace my name upon the sand

Don't buy me chocolates, silk or rings
I do not need expensive things
But wash my hair and rub my feet
Or make me pancakes as a treat

Don't feel the need to dress up fine
And take me out to wine and dine
But light a flame and plant a tree
Or write a tissue poem for me

Perfume

You awaken me
With the light that shines in your eyes
And the gentle breeze of your smile
I rise to embrace your promise
I take your hand

You melt me
With the warmth that glows in your voice
And the fiery burn of your touch
I thaw to enter your river
I drink you in

You intoxicate me
With the taste that smears on your lips
And the heady scent of your hair
I inhale to lap your desire
I breathe you in

You soothe me
With the balm that seeps from your words
And the calming stroke of your sighs
I pause to detect your whisper
I hold you close

You inspire me
With the care that aches in your heart
And the shy wisdom of your ways
I dream to conjure your shadow
I find you home

The Web

As yet another strand is cut
I wonder if it's time
I wonder if the web will hold
Or steadily untwine

And yet we have the choice each day
To spin another thread
To spin a world that's beautiful
Or give in to the dread

For ropes of life and bonds of love
Are possible to weave
Are possible to recreate
If only we believe

Florentine Nights

What sweet surprise, what strange delight
To find myself this Florence night
On wings across the miles to you ...
I wonder if you miss me too

My soul's aglow, my mind's aflame
Among this city's ancient names
Who led the Renaissance in art
And stoked the embers of my heart

A thousand sights, a thousand smells
A thousand stories each one tells
And so I'm wishing you were here
Imagining that you are near

A time too short, an end too soon
A drifting cloud across the moon
A dream beneath the starry skies
The darkest hour before sunrise

Autumn Kisses

autumn puckers
planting kisses on nose and neck
ears and cheeks with cool lips touching
welcoming and refreshing

Love Floats

Love floats
babbling brook of nervous flirtation
swirling swoon of giddy infatuation
turbid torrent of raging passion
melting mist of saturated bliss
emotional eddies of surface tension
umbilical undercurrents of deep connection
futile frothing of angry white-water
wanton whirlpools of selfish indulgence
sobering storms of tempestuous destruction
daydreaming drifting of reflective contentment
steady stream of time-honoured commitment
salvation spring of bubbling rejuvenation
Love floats

Ivy Love

As seasons turn we all must learn
From past love that is dead
Like ivy once was summer-green
Now bleeds to autumn-red
And clings before it fades and falls
To lay a golden bed
Of memories scattered by the wind
And mottled wishes shed
Which decompose to fertile soil
From which new love is fed

The Dream of You

The dream of you in echoed rhymes
The voice of you between the lines
The hum of you across the wires
The spark of you in deep desires

The taste of you on moistened lips
The smell of you on fingertips
The shape of you in gentle light
The feel of you in passion's flight

The sight of you with blissful eyes
The sound of you with breathless sighs
The song of you inside my mind
The dream of you with hearts entwined

Perfect Day

Walking slowly, hand in hand
Beside the gentle river Cam
On past the learnéd halls of time
And college gates where church bells chime

Through market stalls of fresh-baked bread
To corner shops where minds are fed
Along green paths of shady pine
With pause to feast on cheese and wine

Back home, the drum of sultry beat
Of music's sway and passion's heat
Then rest in shadows barely lit
And hugging curves of perfect fit

Too soon the day is at a close
With creamy kiss and pink-blush rose
Against the sky of fading light
A whisper: "no regrets … goodnight"

Chocolate Seduction

Mouth-wateringly tempting ...
When I peel back the wrap on your cocoa skin
And inhale the heady lasso of your scent

Tongue-twistingly scrumptious ...
As I close licked lips around your umber blush
And imbibe the creamy nectar of your bud

Lip-smearingly luscious ...
When I suck the seed of your melting virtue
And swallow the decadent spice of your kiss

Toe-tinglingly piquant ...
As I ride on the swell of your peptic tide
And frolic in the sugar-rush surf of your zest

Heart-meltingly blissful …

When I cradle the curve of your honeyed breath

And repose in the aftertaste of your sigh

A Love That Could Last

How quickly belief turns to doubt
When we've been disappointed before
And how quickly we hold our shield out
When the wounds are still painfully raw

If only our faith was more strong
For no matter the challenge we'll cope
And despite everything that is wrong
Our unfailing redeemer is hope

How quickly delight turns to fear
When we've been disillusioned and caught
And how quickly we tune in our ear
To the cries of past battles we've fought

If only we slowed down and gazed
At the sun and the moon up above
We'd be grateful and truly amazed
By the people and things that we love

How quickly the best turns to worst
When the goal is so nearly in reach
And how quickly we think that we're cursed
When the road leads us into the breach

If only we focused on now
Not the wheel of the eidolic past
And believed in what trust can allow
To emerge – like a love that could last

Galaxies Cart-Wheeling

We make the skies dance and the trees sing
The swans dream and the fields ring
They come alive and flex their voices
Finding joy in simple choices

We make the sun beam and the moon shine
The clouds paint and the stars rhyme
They laugh aloud and skip like children
Letting whirlwinds lift and fill them

We make the clocks whirr and the bells peal
The seeds grow and the earth heal
They join the galaxies cart-wheeling
All because they share our feeling

I Hear You

I hear you in the silence
When all the world's asleep
I hear you tap the window
With pitter-patter feet

I hear you in the whisper
Of trees that gently sway
I hear you in the wave song
Of horse-mane ocean spray

I hear you in the country
In forests and in glens
I hear you in the river
And on the boggy fens

I hear you in the city
Amidst the traffic noise
I hear you on the playground
With laughing girls and boys

I hear you in the spaces
Your visits left behind
I hear you in my heartbeat
And in the poets' rhyme

Turkish Coffee Kisses

Cups of Turkish coffee kisses
Sticky treats of pure delight
Like the lover that he misses
Bitter-sweet on winter nights

Bags of fresh-made salted popcorn
Late-night films in Muswell Hill
Like the magic hour before dawn
Darkness breathes when all is still

Sounds of syncopated beating
Circle rhythms in the round
Like the bloom of flowers fleeting
Bursting bright from underground

Flibbawookie

I'm loofed upon my slumpfry chair
And snugful phrapped without a care
My mind's awhim with pluffly clouds
And wurvly willows floom like shrouds

And there beslind the zub-zib shore
I flond an open majling door
Inverpling me to shwelp into
A wurp-hole that wawoosks me through

To my surprang I chinz to meet
A flibbawookie with floq feet
She prurls into my whyful eyes
And squeebs to lerk me hypnotised

I flonk beneath her quirly gaze
And flerb into the mergly haze
I'm swooked with dreams of virv delight
And flummed with luzzness at first sight!

Broken Dreams

Every time you stir up the embers
I'm left with the burnt-out ash it engenders
And every time you blow up a windstorm
I feel like a wave-tossed ship with sails torn

How I long for the season of calm
When moods do not swing like the ocean tide
And how I long for the plateau of trust
Where words are the vistas in which we confide

But every time you jump to conclusions
I start to believe once more in illusions
And every time you fly off the handle
The flame of my hope snuffs out like a candle

How I long for the showers of rain
That water the roots of our budding affair
And how I long for the sunshine of love
That dispels these dark clouds of gloomy despair

Yet every time you doubt my intention
The seed of my faith re-enters suspension
And every time you leave without farewells
You set my head ringing with more alarm bells

How I long for the cover of night
When darkness revives the heart and feeds the soul
And how I long for the dawning of day
When morning comes and broken dreams emerge whole

Love-Shapes

love comes
in all shapes and sizes -

short and long
right and wrong
with scars and wrinkles
blushes and twinkles
with curves and bulges
and wicked indulges

the twists and bends
of lovers and friends
the mirror reflection
without rejection
never regret
never forget

love comes
in all shapes and sizes

Just Imagine

Just imagine …
A life without each other
Without the smiles and laughter
Without the hand to hold or lips to kiss
No soothing voice to hear
Talking about the day's meanderings
And the mysteries of life and art

Just imagine …
We go our separate ways
Back to our own worlds
Spinning in dark space
Space that is more empty
Because we no longer shine
In each other's night sky

Just imagine …
We become another memory
Something to look back on
To appreciate and yet also regret

Because what we had was good
And now it is merely a shadow
Where the sun might have shone

And all because ...
We somehow lost our faith
In each other and in us
We somehow failed to trust
And to cling to hope's promise
We failed to accept love's call
And to answer "yes!"

Just imagine ...

Island Dreams

You share such beautiful island wishes
That my eyes blink with tears
Sparkling, happy tears
Tears of amazement and wonder
For beauty's smile and love's fecundity in you
For the joy of your risen imagination
Shining like the yellow Moroccan sun

These are the dreams that make life real
These are the words that make my heart beat
Beat in harmony
These are the days of surreal contentment
And the nights of thanking our lucky stars
Of blessing the gods of north and south
For bringing us together, here, now

So as the wind howls and the bare trees
    sway
As the rain spatters my winter window pane
The window on our future
Looks out on spring in a riot of technicolour
With herons sweeping a cerulean sky
And ivy ladders stretched to the moon
Where we lie laughing in Wensleydale
    craters
And scale the lunar summits of love

Listen As She Hums

All the world's in harmony
A thousand beating drums
When I wake up in the morning
And listen as she hums

All the world's a symphony
A thousand chiming gongs
When I'm walking past the bathroom
And hear her singing songs

All the world's a carnival
A thousand samba feet
When I catch her in the kitchen
Hips swaying to the beat

All the world's a canticle
A thousand chanted prayers
When I lie at night beside her
And breathe away her cares

The End (This Time)

This time, my love, we have come to an end
No rivers to cross, no bridges to mend
No daring escape, no final reprieve
This time, my love, I must turn round and leave

We were good together most of the time
When we found our rhythm and spoke our rhyme
But too many doubts have clouded the sky
And now it is time to say our goodbye

This time, my love, there's no ever after
No sunshine kisses or moonlit laughter
No battles to fight or forts to defend
This time, my love, I must leave as a friend

Caterpillar Kisses

We took a walk in London's park
That balmy summer's day
We let off steam
And dared to dream
As stars came out to play
And we were dancing in the dark

We sat beneath the verdant trees
Upon that bench of love
While all around
We heard the sound
Of whispers from above
And so we listened to the leaves

We filled our hearts with wishes
Upon that first bright star
We cast away
Our cares that day
But best of all by far
Were all those caterpillar kisses

My Secret

So you want to know my secret?
The mysterious light in my eyes
And rainbow mist in my smile?

The phantom blush on my brow
And glistening glow on my skin?
The flinted spark of my touch
And flickering flame of my mind?

My secret is simply this:
I have swallowed the sun!
(That fiery orb some call love)

Happy To See You

I am hoping to see you
Happy to be hoping
Hoping to be happy
Happily hoping to see you

I am hopping to see you
Happy to be hopping
Hopping to be happy
Happily hopping to see you

I am happy to see you
Happy to be hoppy
Hoppy to be happy
Hoppingly happy to see you

Scattered Leaves

When shadows drift across the moon
And clouds conspire to block the sun
When stars appear but fade too soon
And all seems lost while nothing's won

I think of you and sense the light
I think of you and feel the glow
Especially in the dead of night
And in the swirls of icy snow

When life's great song is out of tune
And things to do just don't get done
When winter seems to last 'til June
And work becomes a treadmill run

I think of you and feel alive
I think of you and start to smile
Especially when I see us dive
Into a loose leaf litter pile

When rest is short while chores are long
And future visions seem at odds
When even progress still feels wrong
I think of you and thank the gods

Rainbow Mists

I leave today for distant skies
A journey needing no goodbyes
For though I leave my love behind
One happy thought still fills my mind

I know whenever I'm away
My heart reminds me everyday
That she's with me in living dreams
Of glittering stars and moonlit beams

I see the world through what we share
Through all the trials and doubts we bare
There is no place that I can go
Without the stream of our love's flow

So even when I'm on my own
It feels like I am not alone
The sights and sounds of foreign lands
Are rainbow mists in which she stands

Talk To Me!

Talk to me!
The words that bring a wall of silence
A subtle shade of untold violence

Talk to me!
The art of conversation lost
A spell that spreads the chill of frost

The Web of Love

We gather on the beach of life
With surf and sand and sun
To join a husband and a wife
As two hearts become one

We join you in the web of love

And as you journey on your way
Exploring far and near
You'll always have a place to stay
With friends that hold your dear

We hold you in the arms of love

We gather in the maze of time
With twists and turns of fate
To mark this moment as sublime
The meeting of soul mates

We lift you on the wings of love

And when the storm clouds fill the sky
When rain and snow sets in
You'll keep each other warm and dry
Until the sun gets in

We shield you with the hands of love

We gather on the isle of dreams
With blessings from beyond
From distant stars on silver beams
To celebrate this bond

We leave you in the lap of love

Gifts

There are gifts
(So many musely gifts)
That you gave
To me

Gifts I will treasure
Forever –
The view of the bridge
The popcorn curfew –
Forever gifts
I will treasure

Gifts that nobody can take
Away –
The scent of curls
The caterpillar kisses –
Away gifts
That nobody can take

There are gifts
(Such priceless passionate gifts)
That you crafted
For me

Gifts that will live
On and on –
Love letters to Heather
Picture perfect days –
On and on gifts
That will live

Gifts that I can't imagine
Giving back –
A child's poem
Black and white prints –
Giving back gifts
That I can't imagine

There are gifts
(Such sparkling darkling gifts)
That we exchanged
Together

Gifts that were bursting
Surprise –
Islands where fish drum
Houses of stars –
Surprise gifts
That were bursting

Gifts that still echo
Echo echo –
Lessons of flight
Colours in the dust –
Echo echo gifts
That still echo

Then there are gifts
(Such hopeful hope-filled gifts)
That I gave
To you

Gifts that could now become
Worthless –
Because I could not give
The true gift of giving –
Worthless gifts
That could now become

Gifts you will be tempted to
Throw away –
Because you deserve more
So much more than my gifts –
Throw away gifts
You will be tempted to

And then there are gifts
(Such hallowed haunted gifts)
I can never again give
To you

Dance Me

Dance me to an echo's beat
A pulse of tests and time
Dance me to a gecko's feet
Of sticky words and rhyme

Dance me kindly
Dance me blindly
Dance me to the ends

Dance me lightly
Dance me flightly
Dance – forever friends

Dance me to a wicked wind
A swirl of leaves and dust
Dance me even though I've sinned
With angry words and lust

Dance me badly
Dance me madly
Dance me to the ends

Dance me wildly
Dance me childly
Dance – forever friends

Dance me to a different tune
A rhythm soft and slow
Dance me to a waning moon
Of memories' ebb and flow

Dance me surely
Dance me purely
Dance me to the ends

Dance me sadly
Dance me gladly
Dance – forever friends

Gentle On My Mind

You're gentle on my motley mind
Unexpectedly so
You're skipping through my dippy dreams
More than you'll ever know
You're tucked up in my hippy heart
In ways I cannot show
You're gentle on my mossy mind
Unquestionably so

I know I had to leave
Yet still I'm asking why
Was it the fear of waves?
The echo of the sky?
Did phantoms from the past
Cast shadows in my eye?
I know I had to leave
The question remains why?

You're bubbling up in spritely springs
Unpredictably stirred
You're trickling through in synchro songs
I scarcely knew I'd heard
You're sprouting in the cranial cracks
Of conversations blurred
You're bubbling up in sparkling springs
Undeniably stirred

I left you with no choice
With so much left to say
Did I kill the magic?
Did I darken the day?
Did I exit the wings
Three Acts into the play?
I left you with no choice
There's more I want to say

You're gentle on my moorless mind
Inexplicably so
You're twirling round my dappled dreams
And brightening as you go
You're locked safe in my happy heart
Until the day I show
You're gentle on my misty mind
Incandescently so

Dressing Gown

My dressing gown hangs over yours
Content in their fluffy embrace
My sitting room rings with chimes
An echo of your smiling face

Desert Love

My lover's face
Is nothing like the desert plain's
Wide open space

Her rising breast
Cannot compare to sand dune curves
Which never rest

Her diamond ring
Is nothing like the desert rose:
Dull shimmering

My darling's eyes
Are nothing like the sticky dates
With buzzing flies

Her moistened lips
Cannot compare to fresh mint tea's
Sweet steaming sips

Her flashing smile
Is nothing like the sun's bright glare
For endless miles

Yet both seduce me
Boundless in their natural beauty
Both infuse me

Subway Angel

Across the tracks, she glances up and smiles

Her look – a thousand lifetimes long – beguiles

Such mystery in the space between, such light

Such knowing in her eyes I see, such flight

Piercing beams, rattling roar – this is her train

She steps on board, half-waves and smiles again

Our ways diverge; no chance to meet this time

Yet hope remains – this is the Circle Line

Unspoken Words

I'm searching for ways to say what I mean
I'm struggling to speak, and so I have been
Talking in riddles of harbours and birds
While drowning in oceans of unspoken words

Words of reflection and words of regret
Words of forgiveness and words to forget
Words of rejection and words to provoke
Words of star-wishing and words of bright hope

Yet all of these words are hollow beside
The three words of truth I've kept deep inside
The words are "I love you" – yes, I love you still
And there are some promises left to fulfil

I promise to care, to be your best friend
I promise to heal, I promise to mend
The dreams that I crushed, the heart that I broke
The love torn apart by words that I spoke

But can you forgive me? Can you still see
A light on the path to our destiny?
And can you embrace me? Can you refill
The hole that I left? Do you love me still?

Wild Love

For some, love is tame
It is cute and cuddly
Like an adorable pet
Tail-waggingly happy
Purringly content

I have known this tame love
It did not last

Now, I know a different kind of love
A love that is wild
That is nervous and ferocious
Skittish and temperamental
One moment, it trusts enough to approach
The next, it bites the hand that feeds

Such wild love can never be tamed
To cage it is to kill it
Any attempt at domestication
Denies its true nature

Wild love is sometimes fierce
And sometimes it is shy
Yet always it returns
Again and again
Seeking acceptance
Each time a little less afraid
A little less aggressive

Wild love always hurts
But the wounds it inflicts
The pierce of fangs
And the rake of claws
Are nothing but self-defence
For wildness is never malicious

This love comes from the shadows
It is born in the wilderness
It hunts in jungle and canyon
Prowls across desert and plain
Soars over ocean and peak
It is ever vigilant
And breathlessly alive

Wild love can never be conquered
It cannot be bought or won
Only earned, with patience
Patience that teaches understanding
Understanding that builds trust
Trust that creates safety
So that love's caring instincts can take over

In love's wild embrace
Defence gives way to protection
Aggression turns into passion
Fighting becomes playful
Wounds have a chance to heal

Even so, love is never subdued
To love is to risk injury
Flesh wounds are part of living
Bleeding is part of loving
And loving without restraint
Or fear of consequences
Is the way of the wild

Kismet

I see you
In your night of anguish
I see you
In your cave of tears
I see you
In your veil of sadness

Soothing whispers in the midst of anger
Gentle embraces in the midst of pain
Steady vision in the midst of confusion
Patient belief in the midst of doubt

I am by your side
Not leaving this time
I am in your heart
For healing this time
I am for your dreams
In daylight this time

Candles flicker in the midst of darkness
Courage blossoms in the midst of fear
Water quenches in the midst of fever
    Kismet reveals in the midst of love

I love you
No matter what
I love you
No matter where
I love you
No matter why

I Lie Awake

I lie awake and hear your velvet sigh
Across the miles on breaths of midnight air
While blinking stars incant the question why:
Why I am here and you are over there?

I lie awake and see your Cheshire smile
Upon the iridescent wakeful moon
While time is morphed into a melting dial
That tricks and teases like an ancient rune

I lie awake and dream your phantom kiss
Between the sliding doors of mystery
While owls call out to serenade our bliss
And prophesise our echoed history

I lie awake and watch your phosphor glow
Upon the frothing of nocturnal tide
While slumber tussles from the undertow
And whispers: meet me on the other side

The Joining Of Hands

Marriage is like the joining of hands …
Each enfolding the other
A comfortable fit
A voluntary embrace
Yet always two hands
Free to let go
Able to individually express

When two hands touch …
Each senses the needs of the other
And responds
To affirm
To compensate
To share:

The firm handshake of agreement
The gentle squeeze of endorsement
The steady grip of assurance
The uplifting gesture of support

The clenched fists of anger
The desperate claws of pain
The wringing clasp of anxiety,
The sweaty palms of guilt

The loving caress of contentment
The erotic brush of passion
The mutual wave of recognition
The silent fingertip touch of deep
    connection

Marriage is like the joining of hands ...
Each enfolding the other
A comfortable fit
A voluntary embrace
Yet always two hands
Free to let go
Able to individually express

Moment Of Truth

There comes a moment
An empty, aching moment
When words are hollow
Shapeless and ungainly
Unfit for purpose
When metaphors are tired
Bleached and worn out
Dying on lips unuttered
When rhymes are strained
Wrenched and contorted
Twisting straight talk

It is a moment
A helpless, hopeless moment
When bridges and rivers
Do nothing
To unlock the enigma of time
When flames and flowers
Say nothing
To betray the heart's deep secrets
When wings and flight
Know nothing
Worthy of the spirit's journey

In this moment
This broken, naked moment
Music wells up from nowhere
Tremulous and tender
As it rushes into the void
And art explodes from nothing
Luminous and blazing
As it dives into the abyss
Only to be stilled and muted
Dowsed and extinguished
Swallowed by the moment

This is the moment
The white-out, wakeful moment
When all that can be said
Are three simple words
When all that can be felt
Are two hearts beating
When all that can be meant
Is I love you
This is the moment
The moment to live for
The moment of truth

Resonance

The One
Who resonates
In time and in tune
With the subterranean songs
Of Leonard Cohen
And the transcendent words
Of Ben Okri
Has unearthed and unveiled
The deeply buried gateway
To my beating heart
And the long encrypted cipher
To my flighty soul
In step and in space
That resonates
As One

Ambivalence

We think we know
In fact, we're sure
We've never been so sure before
Our feet are firmly planted
On love's rock-steady floor

We think we know
Until we doubt
We let ourselves be turned about
Our level heart gets tilted
And love's storm turns to drought

We think we know
Our mind's hell bent
But in the end we must relent
Our tryst is fated to become
A love ambivalent

Villanelle for Justice

She rages against the fading of light,
Making the world less bitter, less dark:
Her moonlit passion shines out in the night.

When shadows are growing to ominous height;
When justice corrodes and leaves acid marks:
She rages against the fading of light.

Each time that she finds a victim in plight,
She looks for a flash of luminous arc:
Her moonlit passion shines out in the night.

When tyrants defend their merciless right;
When gaps still get wider, contrasts more stark:
She rages against the fading of light.

In stormy dark seas where money is might;
Where bankers and landlords feed like a shark:
Her moonlit passion shines out in the night.

Her fire gives me wings, her love gives me flight,
And helps me to face my fears of the dark:
She rages against the fading of light,
Her moonlit passion shines out in the night.

Hard To Say

It's hard to say 'I love you'
When words have turned to dust
When searing haze inflames the blaze
And chokes the skies of trust

Yet that's the very moment –
Despite the silent blight
When all the best is laid to rest –
My love for you burns bright

It's hard to hug and kiss you
When looks have turned to ice
When every gaze blocks out the rays
Of efforts to be nice

Yet that's the very moment –
Despite the frosty chill
When mutual faith is like a wraith –
My love enfolds you still

It's hard to say 'I'm sorry'
When facing down defeat
When healing ways are like a maze
That's full of dead-end streets

Yet that's the very moment –
Despite still feeling sore
When all the pain is spent in vain –
I love you even more

Through It All

Worlds may collide –
The sky turn to black
Mountains may crumble
The earth shake beneath your feet
Rivers may dry up
The oceans lash out with tidal waves –
And through it all
I will stand beside you

Others may desert you –
Fair weather friends and fickle family
They may walk away
Turn their backs and harden their hearts
They may change their minds
Break their promises and leave –
But through it all
I will be beside you

Storms may come –
The seasons turn to winter
Rain may fall
The sunshine blotted out to grey
Drought may strike
The soil left parched and cracked –
Yet through it all
I will stay beside you

People may talk –
Wag their poison tongues and frown
They may whisper
Spread their rumours like a plague
They may sow their lies
Tut-tut and shake their disapproving heads –
Still through it all
I will be beside you

We may be apart –
Separated by borders and time zones
Oceans may divide us
Whole continents stand in our way
Walls of belief may rise up
Demarcating your world and mine –
And through it all
I will appear beside you

Sickness may visit –
Weaken your will to rise and shine
Time may grow heavy
Drag down your body and fray your mind
Doubts may linger
Gnawing at our love like a cancer –
But through it all
I will remain beside you

Through all of this and more –

Through shining days and unexpected adventures

Through vivid nights and breath-taking summits

Through blissful moments and beauty discovered

Through passion flights and laughter spilled together –

I will be beside you

Because side by side, for now and always

Is where we belong.

Shooting Star

Your shooting star lights up my sky
You are my what, my who, my why
Your trail is bright, I watch it flare
You are my world, my love, my dare

Step Into My Parlour

Step into my parlour
Make yourself at home
Tell me all the dreams you dream
Your fears of things unknown
Let it out, the things you hide
Your deep and inmost trouble
Step into my parlour
But not into my bubble.

Footprints

Laughing, smiling, making jokes
Dreams, desires, fleeting hopes
Not defined, not quite clear
Not quite far, not quite near
Out of reach, close at hand
Sets of prints upon the sand
Follow now and now to lead
Now to give and now to need
Perhaps in time, in time I'll know
Where those footprints are to go.

Dove on the Wind

If you were a dove
I'd be the wind
The wind you so enjoy to journey with
The wind which rides with you to great
    heights
The wind which blows on your face
And reminds you that you are indeed
Free.

Reach Out and Touch

Reach out and touch someone in need
Broken lives, hearts that bleed
Those alone, those in fear
Those in search of someone dear
Give not to them advice nor creed
Reach out and touch someone in need.

Only Love

Only love -
> It's all that matters, all that binds
> All that fulfils, all that finds
> It's all that holds, all that contains
> All that is, all that remains
>> - Only love

Mystery

There is a mystery which is you
A mystery which is me
And a mystery which is you and me.
They are not mysteries to solve
But rather to learn from –
To learn joy and understanding and love.

Loving Thoughts

Send a thought upon a wing
Amidst the pain and suffering
Freely give, don't count the cost
Loving thoughts are never lost.

I Love You Mom

Though I have tried, in song, word and rhyme
I just couldn't capture in the space of a line
How much I love you, how much I care
How when I need you, always you're there
How the freedom you've given is the freedom I need
How you've allowed me to grow, having sown the seeds
How you give of yourself and don't count the cost
How the love that's been gained will never be lost
And never can I harness in the space of one day
All that I feel and all I could say
So you must consider each day of the year
As a celebration of love by the ones you hold dear.

Dad, We Love You

You hear the news, the dice is cast
Nature's cruel sentence passed
What hope there was just seems to fade
The matter's closed, the choices made

It's like the walls are caving in
Your heartbeat aches, your feelings spin
You want to cry, you want to shout
You want to help, you've been shut out

Where's the justice? Who's to blame?
Why does it have to end this way?
Let me speak, this is my cue
Let me in, I love him too!

And feeling hopeless, we stand by
We see your pain, your head's held high
We know in time that you'll pull through
'Til then, remember: we love you.

Kindred Spirits

The sands of time have trickled by
The clouds have shifted in the sky
The sea's between, the earth as well
Strange how Life has weaved her spell

Yet in moments sacred, before inner eyes
Time and Space shed their disguise
And sparks unite to form a flame
Kindred spirits of another plane.

Hunny-Bear

You are my little hunny-bear
The one I love, my only care
So cute and cuddly, and sexy too
My heart belongs to none but you

I love your hunny-bear laugh and smile
Your hunny-bear looks and style
I love the hunny-bear stories you tell
And your hunny-bear bod has me under a
    spell

You are my little hunny-bear
I cherish each moment that we share
So sweet and sassy, so deliciously hot
I'll always be your hunny-pot.

Christmas Wish

My Christmas wish came true last night
When *she* appeared - oh what a sight!
In scarlet gown with edge of snow
And in her hair, a crimson bow
With lingerie of festive red
And playful antlers on her head
With brown doe eyes and luring smile
My heart stopped beating for a while
For she was beauty in all her trappings
Then - oh my God - she removed the wrappings!
Words can't express my childish delight
When my Christmas wish came true last night.

Jealousy

It starts
Like bad indigestion
Churning knots inside my gut
Burning my heart
Clawing

It spreads
Like a creeping cancer
Eating away at my sanity
Crippling my love
Malignant

It crescendos
Like an exploding storm
Unleashing thunderbolts of anger
Flooding with resentment
Destructive

It fades
Like a spent firework
Spitting sparks of sadness
Smoking with regrets
Exhausted.

Cradled by Love

As you lie by my side
With your head on my chest
Our legs intertwined
My hand on your breast
The touch of your fingers
The smile on your face
The world is at peace
Everything's in its place

As the candlelight flickers
Our senses caressed
The music enfolds us
Safe snug in our nest
The cares of the world
Fade away without trace
We are cradled by love
In the soft arms of grace.

Facets

To bind the mind
And tame the flame
To yearn and burn
For pleasure pain

To lust in trust
And sire the fire
To wake and ache
With spent desire

Shades of light
Phases of moon
Rays of night
Rhythms of tune

Circles with edges
Levels with ledges
Thresholds still lure
Curiosities endure

Pressure-fired
In molten crust
Diamonds hide
Within the dust

We see the gem
But only when
We strip away
The hardened clay

To catch the light
Of inner assets
Behold the sight
Of myriad facets.

Wild, Beautiful and Free

Wildness
Is a place in the heart
And with her mane untamed
Passionate
Like the thunder of horses running free
She will always be
A wild woman
To me

Beauty
Is a place in the mind
And with her smile reclaimed
Sensual
Like the moods of the waves on the sea
She will always be
A rare beauty
To me

Freedom
Is a place in the soul
And with her muse unchained
Creative
Like the dance of the breeze
She will always be
A free spirit
To me

Forever
Is a place in the now
And with her gift unnamed
Shining
Like the dew in the sun on the leaves
She will always be
Wild and beautiful
And free.

Truth or Dare

Truth or dare? I hear you say
With impish smile and raised eyebrow
Don't be scared, it's just a game
So be a devil, live for now

Could I refuse? I'm asking you
With tongue in cheek and rolling eyes
For win or lose, you always knew
That I'd be tempted by the prize

Confession was my coward's choice
I swore that I would speak what's true
And so you asked in husky voice:
If I were bound, what would you do?

The image flashed across my mind
A rush of blood made it seem real
The silk and ice, your spanked behind
And pleasures that the fridge concealed

Was that a smirk? It's hard to tell
For still you chose the daring route
I sought my fantasies to quell:
I dared you to a photo shoot

Did you blink? Or even blush
As you began to smile and pose
Then sensually and without rush
One by one removed your clothes

I like to think it was a game
Where we both won and no one lost
For though it kindled a small flame
We never had to count the cost

The embers glow in friendship now
As with each day we trust and share
Yet still we're bound to live our vow
To tell the truth and bravely dare.

Genie Out the Bottle

The genie's out the bottle
I can never put it back
Now I'm ever haunted
By the ghosts of cyberchat

They speak in whispers
I cannot hear
In hidden shadows
They reappear
Leech upon my tender faith
Prey upon my fear

It's not so much their faces
It's more the little spaces
They occupy in her life

As if they meet some need
A hunger I can't feed
As a husband to my wife

I know a little flirting
Is no cause for hurting
The only one I care for

And how can I begrudge her friends
Still I wonder where it ends
Infernal whys and wherefore

It used to be such fun
When we started out as one
Now I'm on the side
Fighting windmills of false pride

I'm in a maze
With dead-end ways
Whatever I do makes it worse
I guess that's the genie's curse

I'm tired of my anger
Tired of my shame
Of my screwed up emotions
Tired of this game

I tell myself to grow up
Stop acting like a child
Yet still the feelings show up
And voices drive me wild

Perhaps all this is penance
A self-inflicted pain
A cross to bear in silence
There's nothing left to gain

The silly thing is this
A kiss is just a kiss
And she has done no wrong

It's only in my head
When I'm lying in my bed
That I hear this doubter's song

So I cling to my belief in love
Rely on hope and trust
Endure the storms of jealousy
Do all the things I know I must

For there may be ghosts in the air
That torment my darkest hour
But she is real and she's with me
Our love has greater power.

Restless Nights

When I wake from restless nights
Weary from nocturnal fights
Your arms reach round to hold me
Your body warm enfolds me
Your tender kisses soothe me
Your gentle whispers move me
Your caring smile revives me
Your loving touch enlivens me
So that by the time you're on your way
I have the strength to face the day.

Letting Go

A meeting
Not of hands but of minds
Not of ground but of finds

A sharing
Not of words but of rhyme
Not of space but of time

A crossing
Not of lands but of arts
Not of skies but of hearts

A soaring
Not of birds but of souls
Not of parts but of wholes

A clashing
Not of swords but of scars
Not of wills but of stars

A shedding
Not of ties but of tears
Not of hopes but of fears

A haunting
Not of ghosts but of threats
Not of truth but of regrets

A changing
Not of stories but of seasons
Not of desires but of reasons

A parting
Not of ways but of means
Not of seas but of scenes

A meeting
Not of beginnings but of ends
Not of strangers but of friends.

Princess

You don't need to wear a crown
Or sip a crystal chalice
No diamond broach
Or gilded coach
To lead me to your palace

You don't need to sweetly smile
Or grace a royal ball
No satin gown
Or trumpet sound
For me to heed your call

You don't need to ride a steed
Or kiss a shining knight
No castle tower
Or magic power
To make me see the light

You don't need a fairytale
Or Disney's happy end
For me to see
You'll always be
A princess and a friend.

She'll Never Know

She'll never know
That I sighed when she left today
And lingered in the mist
Of her presence

She'll never know
That I thought about her today
And gave thanks for blessings
I have received

She'll never know
That I missed her badly today
And just wanted to phone
To say hello

She'll never know
That I had a wild dream today
And she starred in a way
That made me blush

She'll never know
That I fought battles for her today
And we rode to victory
Still together

She'll never know
That I felt loneliness today
And was consoled to think
She'd be home soon

She'll never know
That I saw a flower today
And thought of her face
So beautiful

She'll never know
That I smiled silently today
And heard her faint laughter
Echo in me

She'll never know
Except if I tell her today
And the words I will use
Are I love you.

All I Ever Wanted

All I ever wanted
Was just to make you smile
How was I to know
There can be no smiles
Without the of crush of scowls

All I ever wanted
Was just to make you laugh
How was I to know
There can be no laughter
Without the salt of tears

All I ever wanted
Was just to share your words
How was I to know
There can be no words
Without the twist of fate

All I ever wanted
Was just to be your friend
How was I to know
There can be no friendship
Without the blush of love

All I ever wanted
I have received and more
And now I truly know
There can be no future
Without the dream of us.

Here

Tired
But here
Relaxing in the thought
Of you

Hyper
And here
Bouncing off the walls
With you

Grumpy
But here
Willing to trust my moods
To you

Happy
And here
Wanting to share my joy
With you

Angry
But here
Knowing I will not see the back
Of you

Aroused
And here
Pleased to see its effect
On you

Jealous
But here
Because you should know I care
For you

Apart
Yet here
A bridge across forever joining me
And you.

If You Love Her

If you love her, let her know it
There are countless ways to show it

Make her breakfast, buy her flowers
Hold her through the darkest hours

Take her dancing, do the dishes
Grant her silent secret wishes

Buy teddy bears and bunny rabbits
Cherish her peculiar habits

Read her all-time favourite books
Compliment the way she looks

Go for walks that take a while
Choose a song to make her smile

Feed the birds and talk to cats
Never mock her love of hats

Indulge her fantasies and flirting
Give her comfort when she's hurting

Caress her body, stroke her hair
Fan her passion flame to flare

Trust her when you're not together
Be her shelter from the weather

Share her dreams and favourite things
Give her space to spread her wings

Help her face her doubts and fears
Hold her hand throughout the years

In sacred moments, gently pray it
But don't forget to also say it

You don't have to be a poet
If you love her, let her know it.

Battle Days

in the battle-days ahead

i need strength i don't feel, in the midst of weakness

i need faith i don't hold, in the midst of doubt

i need courage i don't possess, in the midst of fear

i need hope i don't see, in the midst of despair

i am fighting a 100-day war

without any armour

without any plan b

without knowing

if love will survive.

Finally Over

What do you do
When it's finally over?

When trying harder is not enough
When rescues come too late, this time
When you are past the point of no return

It is a cruel and painful place
Suspended in the in-between
Between ending and beginning
Between letting go and touching again
Between leaving and loving
Suspended in the empty void
It is a sad and lonely space

When tears flow without comfort
When numbness and pain collide
When faith and love bleed

When it's finally over
What do you do?

Two Weeks

Two weeks is all it takes
To go from ignorant bliss to knowing pain
From held together to fallen apart
From married to separated

Two weeks is all it takes
To go from fragile trust to shattered faith
From deep honour to lost respect
From lovers to estranged

Two weeks is all it takes
To go from warm embrace to cold rejection
From being in love to being a fool
From touched to deprived

Two weeks is all it takes
To go from nostalgic past to feared future
From steady state to churning change
From one path to two

Two weeks is all it takes
To go from shining hope to shadowed despair
From cruel endings to aching beginnings
From together to alone

Two weeks is all it takes
To go from mountain top to rock bottom
From clear vision to everything blurred
From us to you and I

Two weeks is all it takes
To go from lifelong partner to uncertain friend
From always there to fading presence
From here to gone.

Sad and Blue

I'm mad at you
Boiling, bubbling, spitting, seething
Raging, reeling mad at you

For what you've done
Letting us come undone
With your heartless shun
For twisted means to distorted ends
Where the rule of marriage bends
As you cross the line of friends
For how you disrespected me
All the while neglected me
And finally rejected me
For knowing the pain of bleeding
And yet still being willing
To go ahead with the killing
For all the pathological lies
The dishonesty I despise
And your two-faced disguise
For promises of love forever

Through every kind of weather
And of always staying together
For all the things you could have said
When my jealous wounds bled
And choosing silence instead
For leaving me to guess
While you were creating this mess
And turning us into less
For all the words unspoken
Beneath your smiling token
Which now leave us broken
For making me a spy
Suspecting that you'd lie
And hang me out to dry
For not giving us a chance
Not even a second glance
Before the final dance
For devaluing our past
A union that was meant to last
And that you let go so fast
For how you betrayed me
With your actions degraded me

And finally slayed me

I'm mad at you
But more than that, much more than that
I'm just sad and blue.

Hope

I hope that we can somehow still be friends
That this is not where our journey ends

I hope that as we are painfully torn apart
We have the strength to make a new start

I hope that we can find a way to forgive
Each other and ourselves as we learn to live

I hope that we find the happiness we seek
That we both discover a love we can keep

I hope and wish with each passing day
That in my life you'll always stay.

Comet Sonnet

Ever since meeting, we've taken to flight
Reached for the stars and touched the moon
We've stood together through changing light
From dusk to dawn, from midnight to noon
Time and again, we've crashed to the ground
Caught in a storm, too close to the sun
Our wings have broken, our feet been bound
Our entangled dreams have come undone
Certainty in life's like a blazing comet
Its passage as spectacular as rare
And incredible changes can come from it
If we have the heart to hope and dare
For at last I'm certain and I know it's true:
We were meant to be – and I love you.

Adultery

When I'm gone across the sea
And parted ways amicably
What will remain in memory
Is how you chose adultery

Not all our years of harmony
Nor even words of poetry
Not everything you did for me
But hauntings of adultery

Others judge on what they see
Your gentle smiles and charity
They don't know your true story
Of sordid, sad adultery

And no amount of flattery
Can cancel your capacity
For causing pain and misery
With weapons of adultery

Just as well you don't believe
In karma, hell or purgatory
For you will reap as you deceive
From lying and adultery

Is your feeble conscience eased?
Knowing that you are diseased
A victim of pathology
Of cancerous adultery

You think you're safe in secrecy
That there's no cost to treachery
But all roads lead to injury
On journeys of adultery

So many losses once I leave
But most of all the one I'll grieve
Is your long lost integrity
From choices of adultery.

Love Letter

When I think of our love
I think of feathers and butterflies –
our secret ways of flight
Our love lifts us when we are down
and takes us soaring when we are up

Our love is the magic
that makes the ordinary things in life
extraordinary
not because it is a fantasy
but because it is a way of seeing
the world anew
Our love enchants the mundane
and makes the impossible
seem possible

Our love is a long stretch of beach
with the ocean lapping at our feet
Our love is the footprints
we make together in the sand
and the treasure of shells
we pick up as memories

Our love is the most romantic kind -
with poetry and flowers
with gentle kisses under the stars
and dancing in the rain
Our love is the lasting kind -
with deep roots and resilience
with slow growth and patience
Our love is the burning kind -
with fiery passion and sparks
with glowing embers and heat

Our love is built on a rock of friendship,
with walls that are sturdy
and windows that face the sky
Together we wish on the stars
and soak up the sun
together we dance on the moon
and ride beams of light

Our love pulses with a rhythm
so exhilarating
it is indistinguishable
from our heartbeat

There is no limit
to the songs our love can sing
nor the harmonies our love echoes
Our love resonates
with everything we know
to be soulful

Our love is truth
our love is beauty
our love is freedom

All these things and more I know -
without a shadow of doubt -
because I am in love
and the one I love
is you.

Don't Tell Me That You Love Me

Don't tell me that you love me
But hold my hand
See me smiling
Feel my heartbeat
Hear me breathing
Taste my body

Don't speak of ever after
But be with me
In the moment
Commit to us
For an instant
With all you are

Don't say that you'll be faithful
But make your choice
To be with me
Each time we meet
To share yourself
To be yourself

Don't tell me that you love me
But be my friend
Or my lover
Walk beside me
Til our paths
Diverge once more.

Lingerie Lament

Suspenders drive you mad with hooks
While tight shorts invite longing looks
Braces make you like a clown
While hold-ups never let you down
So strip and throw your cares away
But hang on to that lingerie!

Afterglow

The flash of your smile still glints
The charge of your pulse still flints
The spark of your laugh still bursts
The flame of your voice still thirsts

The wisp of your scent still looms
The blush of your look still blooms
The breeze of your breath still strokes
The spice of your taste still stokes

The sear of your kiss still burns
The mark of your touch still yearns
The heat of your blood still flows
The fire of your heart still glows.

Not Forgotten

For the memories we shared
For the special way you cared
For the seasons turned
And the lessons learned
I'll never forget you

For the double life you led
For the tears you never shed
For the vows you broke
And the lies you spoke
I'll never forgive you.

Je T'Adore

The deepest ocean floor of you
The darkest secret door of you
The furthest sandy shore of you
This much do I adore of you

It's not that you're all perfect
And it's not that love is blind
It's just that you're so worth it
We fit – in heart and mind

I adore you when you're happy
And when you're cold as ice
I adore you when you're angry
And when you're hot as spice

It's not that I'm all-caring
And it's not that love is sweet
It's just that I'm declaring
We make something complete

The softest hidden core of you
The sharpest raking claw of you
The passion in the roar of you
I adore all this and more of you

Say "I Do!"

Say we'll climb to the summit together
Say we'll cherish the view
Say we'll believe in each other together
Forever in faith, say "I do!"

Say we'll wish on the starfish together
Say we'll camp on the moon
Say we'll dream in the orchard together
Forever in hope, say "I do!"

Say we'll fly to the sun together
Say we'll chase after the blue
Say we'll puzzle life's mystery together
Forever in love, say "I do!"

Love Is ...

Love is making mistakes
And fixing them together
Love is raising the stakes
And riding out the weather

We'll conquer the heights
We'll cross stormy seas
We'll defend human rights
We'll walk for the trees

Love is taking what comes
And shaping it together
Love is twiddling our thumbs
And making fun forever

We'll face off attack
We'll march hand in hand
We'll fight back to back
We'll make the last stand

Love is building our dreams
And living them together
Love is chasing sunbeams
And never saying never

We'll wish on the stars
We'll camp on the moon
We'll dance across Mars
To our own loony tune.

With This Ring

With this ring, I set you free
Free to love and free to be
Free to grow and free to dream
Free to spend your life with me

This ring is round and knows no end
It joins a lover and a friend
It joins the past and what's to come
It joins two hearts that beat as one

With this ring, we take our vow
To make the most of here and now
To figure out the what and how
To share the stage and take our bow

This ring is forged with human hands
With gold and jewel from distant lands
So too, we shape our precious love
And chase the blue skies up above.

My Letters

I see you found my letters
My bottle on the seas
At last they reached your shoreline
And whispered on the breeze
They hint at new adventures
And childhood left behind
They tell of magic mysteries
Of worlds you'll seek and find

I see you got my letters
My reasons and my rhymes
I hope they'll light the darkness
And comfort you sometimes
I hope they'll find you smiling
Perhaps they'll make you sigh
But more than that, they'll always cheer
Your future, as you fly

I see you read my letters
My rainclouds and sunbeams
I hope they'll travel lightly
In your memory box of dreams
I hope they'll find you thriving
Perhaps they'll touch your pain
But more than that, they'll always show
Your strength to rise again

I see you kept my letters
My wishes and my fears
I hope they'll find some echo
Of truth across the years
I hope they'll find you happy
No matter your endeavour
But more than that, they'll always say:
You're loved by me forever.

www.ingramcontent.com/pod-product-compliance
Lightning Source LLC
Chambersburg PA
CBHW061948070426
42450CB00007BA/1091